PREHISTORIC!

AFTER THE DINOSAURS

by
David West

A⁺

Smart Apple Media

Published by Smart Apple Media, an imprint of Black Rabbit Books
P.O. Box 3263, Mankato, Minnesota 56002
www.blackrabbitbooks.com

Produced by David West 🧍🧍 Children's Books
6 Princeton Court, 55 Felsham Road, London SW15 1AZ

Designed and illustrated by David West

Special thanks to Dr. Ron Blakey for the maps on page 4 & 5

Copyright © 2014 David West Children's Books

Library of Congress Cataloging-in-Publication Data

West, David, 1956- author.
After the dinosaurs / David West.
    pages cm. -- (Prehistoric!)
Audience: Grades 4 to 6.
Includes index.
ISBN 978-1-62588-086-4 (library binding)
ISBN 978-1-62588-113-7 (paperback)
1. Animals, Fossil--Juvenile literature. 2. Paleontology--Cenozoic--Juvenile literature. I. Title.
QE735.W47 2015
560.178--dc23
                            2013036615

Printed in China
CPSIA compliance information: DWCB14CP
010114

9 8 7 6 5 4 3 2 1

Contents

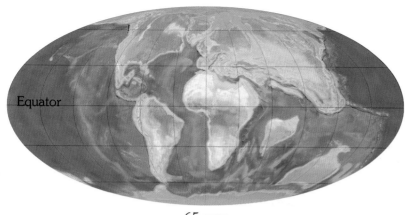

65 mya

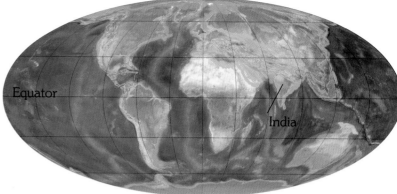

India

35 mya

Terror birds rule the world. (see pages 8–9)

55 mya, global warming raises the Earth's temperature by 11°F (6°C).

India collides with Asia 55 to 45 million years ago.

The **Azolla event** 49 mya brings long-term cooling.

The Cenozoic Era

The era began in the wake of the **Cretaceous– Paleogene extinction event** (K-Pg event) at the end of the Cretaceous that saw the extinction of the dinosaurs. The Cenozoic era is also known as the Age of Mammals because the extinction of many animal groups allowed mammals to diversify.

The Cenozoic era is divided into three periods: the Paleogene, Neogene, and Quaternary. These are further divided into seven epochs: the Paleocene, Eocene, Oligocene, Miocene, Pliocene, Pleistocene, and Holocene.

20 mya

0.65 mya

Equator

Ice sheets

Equator

Isthmus
of Panama

	24			5	2.5	0.15 Today	
OLIGOCENE				MIOCENE	PLIOCENE	PLEISTOCENE	HOLOCENE
				NEOGENE		QUATERNARY	

A global expansion of grasslands, and a regression of tropical broadleaf forests.

South America joins North America through the Isthmus of Panama during the Pliocene.

Ice Age begins 2.58 mya.

LIFE DURING THE CENOZOIC ERA

In the earlier part of the Cenozoic era the world was dominated by the giant terror birds and terrestrial crocodiles. As the forests began to recede and the climate began to cool, mammals took over. The Cenozoic era is full of giant mammals, including **chalicotheres**, **creodonts**, **entelodonts**, saber-toothed cats, **mastodons**, mammoths, and rhinoceros-like Indricotheriums.

The oceans were also home to giant mammals and fish such as *Megalodon*, a shark that grew to 98 feet (30 m).

5

3

2

Giant Snakes

The *Titanoboa* was the largest, longest, and heaviest snake ever to have lived. The warmer climate of Earth during the Paleocene era allowed cold-blooded snakes to grow to much larger sizes than modern snakes.

Unlike modern constrictors that suffocate their prey, scientists think *Titanoboa* hunted by getting close to its prey while submerged in the water, before suddenly leaping out and grabbing it in its massive jaws. *Titanoboa* would have preyed on the crocodile-like *Cerrejonisuchus*

A *Titanoboa* (1) slithers across a tropical swampy landscape. Nearby, an Acherontisuchus (2) is unaware of the giant **predator** as it waits patiently for prey, such as **lungfish** (3). A giant turtle the size of a small car, *Carbonemys* (4), pokes its head above the water.

and *Acherontisuchus*. Some of these **crocodylomorphs** could grow up to 21 feet (6.4 m). It may also have encountered a giant turtle called *Carbonemys*. This giant's shell measured 5 feet (1.5 m) long. It had large, powerful jaws that were capable of devouring crocodylomorphs.

Titanoboa reached a maximum length of 50 feet (15.2 m) and weighed about 2,500 pounds (1,134 kg).

1

Terror Birds

Terror Birds took over from the dinosaurs as the top predators on land. They lived during the Cenozoic, 62–2 mya, mainly in South America. Scientists think that the large terror birds were nimble and quick, reaching speeds of 30 mph (48 km/h).

Gastornis lived during the early to middle Paleogene period in North America and Europe. Scientists think it was an ambush hunter and may have used pack hunting techniques, similar to today's lions, to pursue or

On the edge of the Eocene North American jungle, a pair of *Gastornises* (1) chase after a small herd of *Eohippuses* (2). These early ancestors of the horse relied on speed to evade the fast-running terror birds.

ambush its prey. Similar to the later terror birds of South America, *Gastornis* had adapted to a life on the ground and was completely flightless. Its large beak was curved and sharp at the end, which was ideal for tearing flesh from its victims. These giants preyed on mammals such as *Eohippus*, the early ancestor of the horse.

Gastornis grew to 7 feet (2.1 m) long and weighed up to 300 pounds (136 kg).

Bats and Primates

Icaronycteris was an early bat that lived in North America and Europe. It used **echolocation**, similar to modern bats, to catch insects. Its anatomy suggests it slept hanging upsidedown.

Fossils of *Icaronycteris* have been found in the Green River Formation of North America where there was a group of lakes. Fossils of other animals have been found from the same period, including the early **primate** called *Notharctus*. The body of *Notharctus* is similar to

A group of Icaronycterises (1) leave their roosts in the early evening of an Eocene North America. A group of early primates called *Notharctus* (2) search for insects as a pair of **herbivorous** *Meniscotheriums* (3) run across a fallen tree trunk.

that of a modern lemur. Unlike lemurs, *Notharctus* had a shorter face and forward-facing eyes. It grew to around 16 inches (41 cm) in length, excluding the long tail. It probably ate insects and fruits. Many fossils of a dog-sized, plant-eating mammal called *Meniscotherium* have been found, which suggests they lived in sociable groups.

Icaronycteris measured about 5.5 inches (14 cm) long and had a wingspan of 15 inches (38 cm).

1

Giant

Also known as *Indricotherium* or *Baluchitherium*, *Paraceratherium* was a gigantic, hornless rhinoceros-like mammal living in Eurasia and Asia during the Oligocene epoch. Standing 18 feet (5.5 m) at the shoulder, it is the largest land animal ever to have lived.

Paraceratherium was a browsing herbivore that stripped leaves from trees with its downward-pointing, tusk-like upper teeth. Using its upper lip, it could grab hold of leaves and branches. Its long legs and neck

12

A *Paraceratherium* mother reassures her calf (1) as a group of *Entelodons* (2) approach. These omnivorous pig-like animals grew to 4.4 feet (1.35 m) tall at the shoulders and were capable of eating anything from rotten fruit to dead bodies.

allowed it to browse from the tops of trees where other plant eaters could not reach. Its gigantic size meant that it did not fear predators. Although, its young might have been in danger from packs of *Entelodons* if left unguarded on its own.

Paraceratherium grew to 26.2 feet (8 m) long and weighed 18 tons (16.3 mt).

Horse Rhinos

Megacerops belonged to a group of rhinoceros-like browsers related to horses. Each had a pair of blunt horns on its snout. The males' horns were bigger than the females' horns. These may have been used to butt other males during the mating season.

Megacerops lived in herds and preferred to browse on soft vegetation such as leaves and possibly fruit. It lived in a damp and warm climate among rivers and lakes surrounded by reeds and water bushes.

A volcano erupts in the background as a group of male adult *Megacerops* (1) advance along a dried-up riverbed. A pair of *Andrewsarchuses* (2) look for a weak or juvenile member of the herd in this scene from the middle Paleogene period of North America.

Scientists think it died out due to climate change. Many of the skeletons found belonged to herds that were killed by volcanic eruptions. *Megacerops* was likely to have been hunted by the giant predator, *Andrewsarchus,* which grew up to 13 feet (4 m) long.

Megacerops was about 16 feet (4.9 m) long and weighed about 3.6 tons (3.3 mt.)

Lake Moeris Beast

These prehistoric beasts from the Eocene epoch were members of the elephant family. They looked, however, more like a small hippopotamus with an elongated upper lip. Scientists think they wallowed in lakes and rivers like modern hippos do today.

Moeritherium had long front teeth that were possibly the forerunners of tusks. It may have browsed on soft vegetation such as sea grass and other floating, waterside plants.

16

Moeritheriums (1) wallow in a lake in a tropical forest of Paleogenic North Africa. Early primates called *Apidium* (2) arrive to drink from the river but keep a wary eye out for sharks and crocodiles.

Living alongside *Moeritherium* in what once were the tropical forests of North Africa were early primates called *Apidium*. They lived in trees and moved about like modern squirrel monkeys. Their diet consisted mainly of fruit, and they probably lived in groups. Their average height was around 1 foot (30 cm), and the males were larger than females.

Moeritherium grew to about 2.3 feet (70 cm) high at the shoulder and were about 9.8 feet (2.9 m) long.

1

Rhino Elephant

Another beast from the tropical forests of North Africa was the *Arsinoitherium* that resembled the rhinoceros. Its leg bones suggest it was more like an elephant (especially due to their five-toed feet), rather than a rhinoceros.

Arsinoitherium had a pair of enormous knife-like horns of solid bone that projected from above the nose. A second pair of tiny horns were immediately behind them. The large size and hefty build of

A group of *Arsinoitheriums* (1) feed on plants at the edge of a tropical forest as a *Hyaenodon* (2) eyes them warily. Three **Presbyornithids** (3) fly to their feeding grounds on the coast in this scene from Paleogenic North Africa.

Arsinoitherium were too big for predators. However, carnivorous creodonts such as *Hyaenodon* may have preyed on the young or unhealthy. Despite their name, these large creatures are not related to hyenas.

Arsinoitherium grew to 9.9 feet (3 m) long, 5.9 feet (1.8 m) tall at the shoulders, and weighed around 2.5 tons (2.3 mt).

19

Terror Pig

One of the scariest-looking predators from prehistory roamed the grassy plains of Oligocene North America. It was called a *Daeodon,* also known as *Dinohyus,* which means "Terror Pig."

At 5.9 feet (1.8 m) at the shoulder, *Daeodon* was a monstrous, boar-like creature that ate plants and animals. It probably **scavenged** on the kills of other animals using its powerful jaws to break and crush bones to get at the rich marrow inside. It may also have hunted smaller

A group of *Daeodons* (1) catch the scent of a wounded animal on the grasslands of the North American Oligocene. In the background, a herd of *Menocerases* (2) are spooked by *Miohippuses* (3) galloping away from danger.

mammals such as the pony-sized *Menoceras* or the 4-feet-long (1.2 m) *Miohippus*. The *Miohippus* was one of the most successful prehistoric horses of the Oligocene epoch. Other prey might have included the small **camelid**, *Stenomylus,* and an extinct type of beaver called *Palaeocastor.*

Daeodon grew up to 12 feet (3.7 m) long and weighed 2,200 pounds (998 kg).

2

Strange Elephants

Deinotherium was a large prehistoric relative of the modern-day elephant. It had a smaller trunk and downward curving tusks attached to the lower jaw. It may have used the tusks to dig around in soil for roots and tubers or to strip bark from tree trunks.

Deinotheriums lived in parts of Asia, Africa, and Europe. The last populations of *Deinotherium* held out in Africa until approximately one million years ago.

A family of *Deinotheriums* (1) approach a watering hole in the grasslands of Neogene Europe. A male and female *Platybelodon* (2) wait impatiently on a rocky ledge for their turn to drink.

Another relative of the elephant was living at the same time. *Platybelodon* was not as big, growing only to 10 feet (3 m) long. It is popularly known as a shovel tusker because of its strangely shaped mouth. Using its lower teeth, it also stripped bark from trees for food.

Deinotherium was about 16 feet (4.9 m) in length and weighed up to 10 tons (9.1 mt).

23

2

Cats and Bears

Also known as the saber-toothed tiger, the *Smilodon* was a top predator of the Quaternary period of North and South America (see also pages 26–27). It was not a member of the modern cat family and died out approximately 10,000 years ago.

Smilodon did not hunt as the modern lions and leopards, who grab the throat of their prey until it is suffocated. Instead, it ambushed its prey, bringing it down with its powerful front legs. It used its long, saber-like

A group of *Smilodons* (1) chase off a lone terror bird, *Titanis* (2). This scene is from North American Pleistocene. In the foreground, a group of short-faced bears called *Arctodus* (3) rest around a shallow pond.

teeth to stab the victim in the throat, which would have killed it very quickly. It hunted large mammals such as bison, camels, ground sloths, wild pigs, horses, and mastodons. It may have encountered the very large *Arctodus*, which weighed 1 ton (900 kg). These massive bears competed for the same food and may have stolen the kills from *Smilodons*.

Smilodon grew up to 6 feet (1.8 m) and 500 pounds (227 kg).

Giant Sloths

Megatherium was an enormous elephant-sized ground sloth that lived in Central and South America. It lived in woodland and grassland environments until as recently as 10,000 years ago.

Megatherium walked on all fours on the sides of its feet. Its claws prevented it from putting its feet flat on the ground. Rising on its back legs, it used its tail to form a tripod. Using its long arms with curved claws, it pulled down the branches with the most leaves.

26

A group of *Smilodons* (1) try to fight off a *Megatherium* (2) who is intent on stealing their half-eaten prey, a *Macrauchenia* (3). In the background, armadillo-like **glyptodonts**, *Doedicuruses* (4) feed on vegetation.

Scientists think it had a long tongue, which it used to pull leaves into its mouth, similar to a modern tree sloth. While mostly herbivorous, *Megatherium* may have used its size and strength to take over the kills of the saber-toothed cat, *Smilodon*. It might also have fed on glyptodonts.

Megatherium grew to 20 feet (6.1 m) long and weighed around 4 tons (3.6 mt).

1

Ice Age Monsters

Due to frozen bodies with skeletons, stomach contents, and now liquid blood, as well as cave paintings, scientists know more about the woolly mammoth than any other prehistoric animal.

To keep out the cold, the coat of a woolly mammoth had a layer of hairs 1 foot long (30 cm), and an undercoat of shorter hairs. Its ears and tail were small, which minimized frostbite and heat loss. Its long, curved tusks were used for fighting, foraging, and clearing snow to get

A herd of woolly mammoths (1) travel past a pair of woolly rhinos, *Coelodonta* (2) as they clear snow with their long horns to get at the vegetation underneath in this ice age scene from Eurasia.

at the grass underneath. Like the woolly mammoth, the woolly rhino adapted to the cold with a furry coat. Depicted by human ancestors in cave paintings it became extinct at around the same time.

Woolly mammoths grew up to 11 feet (3.4 m) tall and weighed 6 tons (5.4 mt).

Animal Listing

Other animals that appear in the scenes.

Acherontisuchus
(pp. 6–7)
dyrosaurid
21 feet (6.4 m) long
Africa, Asia, Europe,
North America,
South America

Andrewsarchus
(pp. 14–15)
mammal
13 feet (4 m) long
Asia

Apidium
(pp. 16–17)
primate
1 foot (30 cm) long
North Africa

Arctodus
(pp. 24–25)
tremarctine bear
7 feet (2.1 m) long
North America

Carbonemys
(pp. 6–7)
turtle
5 feet (1.5 m) shell
North America

Coelodonta
(pp. 28–29)
rhinocerotid
12.5 feet (3.8 m)
long
Europe, North Asia

Doedicurus
(pp. 26–27)
glyptodont
13 feet (4 m) long
South America

Entelodon
(pp. 12–13)
entelodont
4.4 feet (1.3 m) tall
Europe, Eurasia,
Asia

Eohippus
(pp. 8–9)
equid
2 feet (61 cm) long
North America

Hyaenodon
(pp. 18–19)
creodont
5 feet (1.5 m) long
Africa, Asia, Europe,
North America

Macrauchenia
(pp. 26–27)
mammal
9.8 feet (3 m) long
South America

Megalodon
(pp. 4–5)
cartilaginous fish
98 feet (30 m) long
Oceans

Meniscotherium
(pp. 10–11)
mammal
1 foot (30 cm) long
North America

Menoceras
(pp. 20–21)
rhinocerotid
5 feet (1.5 m) long
North America

Miohippus
(pp. 20–21)
equid
4 feet (1.2 m) long
North America

Notharctus
(pp. 10–11)
primate
16 inches (41 cm)
long
Europe, North
America

Platybelodon
(pp. 22–23)
proboscid
10 feet (3 m) long
Europe, North
America

Titanis
(pp. 24–25)
phorusrhacid
8 feet (2.4 m) tall
North America

Glossary

Azolla event Taking place about 49 million years ago, blooms of the freshwater fern Azolla sank to the stagnant sea floor in the Arctic Ocean. This massive reduction of carbon dioxide from the atmosphere helped transform the planet from a "greenhouse Earth" state to the icehouse Earth it has become.

camelid A member of a group of mammals that includes the camel.

chalicotheres A group of herbivorous mammals with long forelimbs and short hind limbs living in North America, Europe, Asia, and Africa during the early Eocene to early Pleistocene.

creodonts Members of a group of meat-eating mammals that lived from the Paleocene to the Miocene.

Cretaceous-Paleogene extinction event A mass dying-off of approximately three-quarters of plant and animal species on Earth—including the dinosaurs.

crocodylomorphs Members of an important group of reptiles that includes the crocodiles.

echolocation The way some animals navigate and hunt by emitting sound and using its echoes to locate and identify the objects around.

entelodonts A member of a family of pig-like omnivores, sometimes called hell pigs or terminator pigs, that lived from the middle Eocene to early Miocene.

equid A member of a family of hoofed mammals, which includes modern horses.

fossils The remains of living things that have turned to rock.

glyptodont A member of a family of large, heavily armored mammals that includes the modern armadillo.

herbivorous Feeding on plants.

lungfish A freshwater fish that is able to breathe air with the use of its lungs.

mastodons A member of a group of mammals related to elephants and lived in North and Central America during the late Miocene or late Pliocene.

omnivorous Feeding on both meat and plants.

phorusrhacid A member of the family of large carnivorous flightless birds known as terror birds.

predator An animal that hunts other animals for food.

presbyornithids A member of a family of waterbirds with a global distribution that lived until the early Oligocene period.

primate Any mammal of the group that includes the lemurs, lorises, tarsiers, monkeys, apes, and humans that first appeared during the late Paleocene.

proboscid A member of the trunked mammal family.

scavenge To feed off dead animals.

tremarctine bear A subfamily of bears that includes the modern-day Spectacled Bear.

Index